TURNING POINTS

THE GREAT RECESSION

BY KATE RIGGS

CREATIVE EDUCATION • CREATIVE PAPERBACKS

Published by Creative Education and Creative Paperbacks
P.O. Box 227, Mankato, Minnesota 56002
Creative Education and Creative Paperbacks are imprints of
The Creative Company
www.thecreativecompany.us

Design and production by The Design Lab
Art direction by Rita Marshall
Printed in China

Photographs by Alamy (Norma Jean Gargasz), Corbis (Bettmann,
Matthew Cavanaugh/epa, Najlah Feanny, Porter Gifford, Ashley Gilbertson/
VII, LM Otero/AP, JUSTIN LANE/epa, James Leynse, TANNEN MAURY/
epa, Minnesota Historical Society, FRANK POLICH/Reuters, MICHAEL
REYNOLDS/epa, H. Armstrong Roberts/ClassicStock, Tony Savino, Ramin
Talaie, Underwood & Underwood, Jan Woitas/dpa, JIM YOUNG/Reuters),
Dreamstime (fstockfoto), Newscom (DOOLEY JOHN/SIPA, RICHARD B. LEVINE)

Library of Congress Cataloging-in-Publication Data
Riggs, Kate.
The great recession / Kate Riggs.
p. cm. — (Turning points)
Includes bibliographical references and index.
Summary: A historical account of the Great Recession, including the causes
of the economic downturn, the role played by the Federal Reserve and other
government offices, and the lingering aftermath.

ISBN 978-1-60818-749-2 (hardcover)
ISBN 978-1-62832-345-0 (pbk)
ISBN 978-1-56660-784-1 (eBook)
Recessions—United States—History—21st century—Juvenile literature. /
Global Financial Crisis, 2008-2009—Juvenile literature. / Financial crises—
United States—History—21st century—Juvenile literature. / United States—
Economic conditions—2009—Juvenile literature. / United States—Economic
policy—2009—Juvenile literature.

HB3743.R54 2016
330.973/0931—dc23   2016002552

CCSS: RI.5.1, 2, 3, 8; RI. 6.1, 2, 4, 7; RH.6-8.3, 4, 5, 6, 7, 8

First Edition HC 9 8 7 6 5 4 3 2 1
First Edition PBK 9 8 7 6 5 4 3 2 1

Cover, main image: American currency at a federal printing facility
This page: The trading floor of the Chicago Board of Trade

TABLE *of* CONTENTS

Introduction, 5

Chapter One | Supply and Demand   7
Pointing Out: The Panic of 1907, 8
Pointing Out: Leading the Federal Reserve, 12

Chapter Two | Bursting the Bubble   17
Pointing Out: Too High a Cost, 21
Pointing Out: From South Carolina to the Fed, 23

Chapter Three | Off the Cliff   26
Pointing Out: Strategic Takeovers, 30
Pointing Out: Down around the World, 32

Chapter Four | Crawling toward Recovery   34
Pointing Out: New Rules for Finance, 40
Pointing Out: Who's Responsible?, 43

Timeline, 44
Endnotes, 45
Selected Bibliography, 46
Websites, 47
Index, 48

Dressed as Robin Hood, who famously stole from the rich to give to the poor, protesters expressed their frustration with government bailouts of large financial corporations.

On Thursday, September 18, 2008, the secretary of the United States Treasury and the chairman of the Federal Reserve walked into the U.S. Capitol. They sat down in the Speaker of the House's office. Republicans and Democrats from both the House and the Senate were gathered there. Federal Reserve chairman Ben Bernanke told the lawmakers that Congress needed to authorize a massive spending bill. Treasury secretary Hank Paulson said, matter-of-factly, "Unless you act, the financial system of this country and the world will melt down in a matter of days." Bernanke warned, "If we don't do this tomorrow, we won't have an **economy** on Monday." The lawmakers were stunned into silence. They knew these were not empty threats by people inclined to exaggeration. They had seen the crises tumbling one after another, like bowling pins, for months.

The longest downturn since World War II, the Great **Recession** became a defining moment in the early 21st century. For 18 months (December 2007–June 2009), the American economy stumbled through losses in trade and production, increases in unemployment, declines in housing values, and one crisis after another in the financial sector. The aftershocks soon spread around the globe, making a complete recovery even harder to achieve.

CHAPTER ONE

SUPPLY AND DEMAND

I n the U.S., the economy relies on many things. People buy products. They pay for services. Bankers take care of people's money. **Stock** traders invest in the markets. And the federal government watches over everyone. Or at least, it's supposed to. The Federal Reserve was created to be the nation's central bank in 1913. Its job was to stabilize banks around the country by controlling the overall money supply. The "Fed" was not meant to look after private companies. The govern- ment figured other financial firms could look after themselves. In time, though, financial companies grew larger and more powerful than expected.

Before the Fed was established, bank- ing panics were common. Traditional banks did not necessarily keep enough money on hand to be able to give it back to their cus- tomers. They invested in the stock market

U.S. Federal Reserve, Washington, D.C.

The Fed issues new bills and coins each year to replace the damaged and worn money it has pulled out of circulation.

and other places. If a bank lost too much money in the stock market, customers became nervous. They wanted to pull their money out of the bank. But if the bank couldn't pay back all the money, it went out of business. One bank's failure often sparked others'. Panic ensued.

Such a disastrous panic occurred in 1907 that Congress started studying the banking system the following year. Led by senator Nelson Aldrich, a group of bankers eventually came up with a plan for a central bank. Congress then used this plan to create the Federal Reserve. Although the Fed is *the* central bank, it is itself made up of 12 banks. These banks are in Boston, New York, Philadelphia, Cleveland, Richmond, Atlanta, Chicago,

POINTING OUT

THE PANIC OF 1907

One hundred years before the Great Recession, another serious financial crisis took place. The U.S. was already experiencing a period of recession in 1907. To make matters worse, some businessmen schemed to manipulate the stock price of shares in a copper company. They hoped to make a lot of money and gain control over the copper stock. Instead, the shares lost significant value and caused related banks and firms to go bankrupt. Famed New York banker James Pierpont Morgan worked with other company presidents to keep Wall Street afloat by pooling their own money.

During the Panic of 1893, people gathered in large crowds outside banks, anxious to withdraw their money before the bank closed.

MULLERS
EMPLOYMENT
AGENCY
1 FLIGHT UP
OTTO BECK, Lic.

ADMISSION FRE

Throughout the Great Depression, employment agencies were overwhelmed by people looking for work.

St. Louis, Minneapolis, Kansas City, Dallas, and San Francisco. They are called reserve banks because they hold the reserves, or available funds, for their local member banks. The idea was to have the reserve bank act as "lender of last resort" if a local bank ran short on money. The purpose was to prevent the types of panics that had happened before.

Approximately one-third of **commercial** banks joined the Federal Reserve System. Members were able to borrow money from the Fed. They purchased stock in their local reserve bank. They agreed to follow certain rules. Nonmember banks did not have the same protections—or restrictions. The majority of American banks stayed outside the Federal Reserve System.

During the 1920s, the American economy grew. Americans borrowed money from banks to buy houses. They borrowed money to invest in stocks. The Fed raised **interest** rates to try to slow the borrowing. But then stock prices started to go up and down, and people got nervous. They started selling off their stocks, but the stocks were losing value quickly. Around the same time, there was a widening gap between the richest Americans and everyone else. In 1928, the richest 1 percent made more than 23 percent of the income in the U.S. The people who were doing all the purchasing, though, were in the middle class. And the way they were paying for large purchases was through debt—the loans they took out.

Once the stock market crashed in October 1929, the money that had been invested there essentially disappeared. People lost their life savings. They lost their homes when their banks failed. Many lost their jobs, too. The leaders of the Fed allowed troubled banks to fail. They thought that would strengthen the banking system in the end. For all the panics that had happened before, no one had ever seen anything like the **Great Depression**.

LEADING THE FEDERAL RESERVE

At the top of the Federal Reserve System is a Board of Governors. Its 5 to 7 members are appointed by the U.S. president to serve 14-year terms. The chairman and vice chairman have four-year positions and can be reappointed. Fed governors supervise the Federal Reserve banks, oversee the national banking system, and keep an eye on the general state of the economy. The Board's frequent meetings are usually open to the public, unless private financial concerns need to be discussed. Nearly 2,000 people work on staff for the Board of Governors.

In the 1930s, many banking reforms were made. The Federal Deposit Insurance Corporation (FDIC) was created, and banks backed by the FDIC could promise their customers that their money would be protected (up to a certain amount). The structure of the Fed changed, too. Its Board of Governors in Washington, D.C. was given more control. The positions of chairman and vice chairman replaced posts previously held by U.S. Treasury Department officials. Not until 1951 was the Fed able to act independently of the president and Treasury Department, though.

The lessons of the Great Depression had a lasting effect. However, some were soon forgotten in the economic boom that followed World War II. Times were good for many Americans. From the late 1940s through the late 1960s, wages increased, workers unionized, Social Security, Medicare, and

Before the Board of Governors was restructured, the Treasury secretary also served as the chairman of the Federal Reserve Board of Governors.

As the unemployment rate soared above 9 percent in the early 1980s, the size and frequency of demonstrations in the nation's capital increased.

GIVE PEOPLE DIGNITY GIVE THEM JOBS

OUR JOBS FLEW AWAY, LETS SEND REagan FLYING!

SENATOR!!...

STAY THE COURSE LOSE EVERYTHING!

Union Jobs Union wages

HOW YOU UNE BEN UE 6

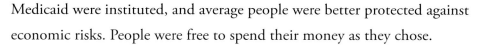

Medicaid were instituted, and average people were better protected against economic risks. People were free to spend their money as they chose.

Starting in the late '60s, the Fed allowed the supply of money to grow excessively. **Inflation** rose steeply. The unemployment rate also went up. By mid-1980, inflation neared 14.5 percent, and unemployment was about 7.5 percent. Part of the Fed's job was to keep both levels at or below 3 percent. The prevailing theory was that a moderately high level of inflation would keep unemployment down. Yet this was proven wrong throughout the period known as the Great Inflation. To make matters worse, wages were beginning to drop off for middle-class Americans. Stagnant wages were at first offset by more women joining the workforce, and then by everyone working longer hours (or more jobs). But as people went into debt to continue financing a similar level of spending as they had enjoyed decades before, their empty purchasing began to test the limits. The economy rebounded in the short term, but its relative stability from the mid-1980s to 2007 proved to be a mirage.

Under Fed chairman Alan Greenspan, the Fed's role had expanded in the late 1990s. It began to watch over financial holding companies in addition to banks and investment firms. Greenspan took a light hand when it came to enforcing laws on the financial sector, believing regulation could typically do more harm than good. A few years later, critics wondered whether the Fed had really done its job as regulator. Journalist Andrew Ross Sorkin questioned, "What did Greenspan and his Fed know, and when did they know it? What did they do—or fail to do—about it? What did the Fed miss? What could the Fed have done differently to prevent the Great Panic or, at least, to minimize the damage the panic did to the economy?"

RPORATED
JUMBO
LOANS
4.5% OR
Conforming
5 YEAR
FIXED LOANS
4.696 A.P.R.
AS LOW AS
RATES SUB. TO CHANGE
5.125%
5.404 (A.P.R.)

CHAPTER TWO

BURSTING THE BUBBLE

One source of blame for that Great Panic, which became the Great Recession, can be traced to 2001. A brief recession that year caused the Fed to lower interest rates. Banks can loan more money when interest rates are low, and people often take advantage of those rates to secure mortgages on homes. Correspondingly, the demand for houses at such low interest rates soon increased. With more demand, sellers were able to increase their prices. The value of houses became overinflated, and many sold for much more than they were actually worth. Many banks then jumped on the housing bubble bandwagon by offering subprime loans. These loans were aimed at people who had poor **credit** histories. Subprime loans offered the ability to get mortgages with little money down at the outset but often had higher interest rates tacked on.

In the financial world, subprime loans were chopped up into other **securities**. These securities were traded and shared among hundreds and thousands of parties. So the loans weren't kept by any one bank—they were spread out to many. And thanks to changes in laws and regulations in the early 2000s, investment banks became much bigger players in the overall banking system. When subprime loans were found to be incredibly risky and bad, it affected much more than a single financial institution. After a major

A mortgage company advertised jumbo loans in 2008, shortly after loan limits were increased in an effort to stimulate the housing market.

subprime mortgage company filed for **bankruptcy** in 2007, many banks stopped issuing the loans. With fewer loans available, the demand for houses dropped, and home prices fell, too. When people tried to sell their houses, they couldn't get as much money as what they owed for the mortgage. So the bank from which they obtained the mortgage took over the sale in **foreclosure**. This type of sale enables banks to make back most of the money owed them, but it doesn't help the homeowner purchase another house.

Ben Bernanke, who had taken over as Fed chairman in 2006, did not at first see the connection between the housing market collapse and the economic troubles that followed. In a June 2007 speech, he declared, "at this point, the troubles in the subprime sector seem unlikely to seriously spill over to the broader economy or the financial system." Because of the way that big Wall Street firms such as JP Morgan and Lehman Brothers packaged those subprime loans with other **derivatives**, though, spillover was indeed likely. At that time, there was $14 trillion in the U.S. mortgage market. Of that, $2 trillion came directly from subprime mortgages. Yet the nature of the way investment banking worked made that segment more significant. The loans that were made to homeowners were sold to other investors and insurers. Many more outfits thus had a stake in the success or failure of those loans. For the

The number of homes in foreclosure continued to climb until 2011, when foreclosures fell by 34 percent from the year before.

Locks are changed on repossessed homes, and windows and doors are often boarded up with plywood to prevent trespassers and vandalism.

POINTING OUT

TOO HIGH A COST

In 2008, more than one million people lost their homes to foreclosures. That represented a 63 percent rise in foreclosures over the previous year. As home prices continued to fall and loans became scarcer, the housing bubble burst. Part of the problem with the subprime loans that were popular before the crisis was that they had adjustable rates. They began at one interest rate but could be changed by the lender (the bank or mortgage company) later on. Once the rates went too high for the homeowner to make the payments, the risk of foreclosure kicked in.

most part, these outfits were outside the system of Fed-protected commercial banks.

The Fed was not alone in its initial diagnosis. American economists in general tend to have faith in the ability of markets to check themselves. Because the economy continued to grow through the early 2000s without **deflation**, it didn't seem as though a crisis was imminent. What even the regulators such as the Fed missed was the greedy risk that drove financial institutions to continue that growth. People did not worry about *saving* money because it seemed like a better idea to make it while prices were low.

By August 2007, trouble in the housing market began to affect both credit markets and banks. Usually, when there's a problem in the credit market, people can borrow from banks. The reverse is true when the trouble originates in the banking sector. However, when neither one is stable enough to lend funds, the system screeches to a halt. Four months later, the Great Recession began.

With banks in crisis mode, the Fed stepped in. As "lender of last resort," it became the first responder to the emergency. It lowered the interest rate to zero. It lent emergency funds for a few days or weeks until banks could raise enough cash on their own. It bought at a discount IOUs that businesses had given banks. Soon enough, it became painfully clear that these measures wouldn't be enough to stem the tide. Too many institutions were in need. Bernanke and the Fed realized they would need to do more than a central bank was intended to do.

At the Fed's reserve bank in New York, president Timothy Geithner was receiving panicky messages from Wall Street bankers. Rather than supervise them, Geithner was being asked to save them. The global investment bank known as Bear Stearns was in particular trouble. Bear traded with 5,000 other firms. It had 750,000 derivatives contracts. It was extremely interconnected, and it was in danger of declaring bankruptcy.

Despite lowered rents and shorter leases, stores and other businesses continued to close throughout the worst days of the recession.

FROM SOUTH CAROLINA TO THE FED

According to Ben Bernanke's mother, "One of his teachers said you could put him in a dark closet and he'd still learn." Former Fed chairman Bernanke was always an outstanding student. After growing up in a small South Carolina town, he attended Harvard and then went on to graduate studies at the Massachusetts Institute of Technology. He taught economics before joining the Board of Governors in 2002. During his tenure as Fed chairman (2006–14), he used his background in teaching to help others understand the issues at play in the Great Recession.

On the day Bear Stearns was supposed to file for bankruptcy (Friday, March 14, 2008), Geithner organized a 6:00 A.M. conference call among himself, Bernanke, Fed vice chairman Donald Kohn, Fed governor Kevin Warsh, Treasury secretary Hank Paulson, and a few others. Within two hours, the group had come to a consensus that they would make a $30-billion loan to Bear Stearns, via JP Morgan. It was then up to Bernanke, Kohn, Warsh, and the only other available Fed governor, Randy Kroszner, to formally approve the loan by vote. Although the original Federal Reserve Act called for five votes to approve

JP Morgan purchased Bear Stearns at a deep discount—Stearns' stock prices were previously $84 a share.

the lending of Fed funds to any institution other than a regular bank, a more recent change in the law provided that, as long as the available governors were unanimous, loan approval could be achieved if it was "to prevent, correct, or mitigate serious harm to the economy or the stability of the financial system of the United States." By the end of the weekend, though, the Fed and JP Morgan had agreed to a new deal in which the Fed would subsidize JP Morgan's proposed $236-million acquisition of Bear Stearns. (Morgan eventually bought Bear Stearns for $10/share instead of $2.)

The Fed board (all five of them this time) met on Sunday afternoon to approve the deal. This vote essentially enabled the Fed to lend directly to other investment banks. In doing so, the Fed hoped to avoid the type of financial panic that the threat of Bear Stearns' bankruptcy had caused. Critics of the Fed's action thought that this would open the door to other institutions taking even greater risks because they would expect the Fed to rush in and save them. At an April 2008 meeting of the Senate Banking Committee, Kentucky senator Jim Bunning asked, "What's going to happen if a Merrill or a Lehman or someone like that is next?" What, indeed?

CHAPTER THREE

OFF THE CLIFF

ehman Brothers was the fourth-largest investment bank in the country. Like Bear Stearns, it was also in rough shape. Unlike Bear Stearns, though, it tried for many months to mask its weaknesses. The same month JP Morgan bought Bear, Lehman had started raising capital. They even reached out to famed Berkshire Hathaway CEO Warren Buffett for help, but Buffett had had too many concerns about Lehman's 2007 annual report; he would never invest in anything if he had too many questions. So Lehman moved on, looking for money elsewhere. But help was nowhere in sight.

Meanwhile, officials from the Fed, Treasury Department, and Securities and Exchange Commission (SEC) were ordered to appear at hearings before the Senate Banking Committee. Although bailing out financial institutions wasn't unheard of, it had never happened exactly the way the Bear Stearns deal had gone down. In the late 1980s and early 1990s, Congress had approved the closing of more than a thousand savings and loan associations. This had ended up costing about $150 billion. Privately, Paulson and Bernanke felt it would have been flat-out impossible to get Congress to act on any meaningful financial regulatory changes in an election year. So

Formerly known as the Bear Stearns Building, 383 Madison Avenue is now owned and occupied by JP Morgan.

The Federal Housing Finance Agency (FHFA) was created in 2008 to supervise Fannie Mae and Freddie Mac.

they hadn't even tried to go that route with Bear Stearns. In April 2008, the Fed, Treasury, and SEC all defended the Bear Stearns deal as a one-off act, hopefully never necessary to repeat.

A new crisis was soon on the horizon. This time, it involved the federal mortgage companies Fannie Mae and Freddie Mac. The two corporations had been borrowing at low interest rates all over the world and had amassed unforeseen amounts of debt. Foreign investors assumed the U.S. government would back that debt, considering Fannie Mae and Freddie Mac were government-sponsored. What many people did not realize was that the companies' debt was even greater than the federal government's! (In March 2007, before the housing bubble burst, it was $5.2 trillion versus the federal debt of $4.9 trillion.) Once the housing crisis picked up, the companies'

Treasury secretary Hank Paulson, Fed chairman Ben Bernanke, and SEC chairman Christopher Cox testified before Congress in July 2008.

involvement in risky mortgage practices—such as the subprime loans—made them completely unsustainable. This time, Paulson went to Congress for help. On July 13, 2008, he asked Congress to give Treasury unlimited lending power or "to invest taxpayer money in their shares if they needed capital." The Fed made assurances that it would lend the money to Fannie and Freddie if need be. The plan eventually became one of conservatorship—with the government taking over and replacing their CEOs. "The Fannie/Freddie thing was a brilliant operation, absolutely necessary," Bernanke said later. "It stabilized an important part of the financial system at a critical time."

As Congress was raising the **debt ceiling** to accommodate the absorption of Fannie Mae and Freddie Mac, Lehman Brothers was desperately hunting for someone to buy the firm. They were running out of possibilities. Finally, on September 12, 2008, Paulson and Geithner met with CEOs of the 20 largest New York banks and investment houses to see what could be done with Lehman Brothers. The Fed did not want to post bail for Lehman, especially since it seemed that wouldn't be the end of the trouble, and it would have taken massive sums to do so. Lehman's competitors had problems of their own; no one wanted to take on Lehman's liabilities as well. Three days later, Lehman filed for bankruptcy, and the markets reacted severely. As former Fed vice chairman Alan Blinder remarked later, "After Lehman went over the cliff, no financial institution seemed safe. So lending froze, and the economy

POINTING OUT

STRATEGIC TAKEOVERS

When businesses are failing, that can be the perfect time for them to be bought out. That's what the Fed had hoped would happen with Lehman Brothers. However, no other company wanted to deal with all the problems Lehman had stacked against it. The strategy worked for others, though: Bank of America bought Countrywide Financial in July 2008, and JP Morgan purchased Bear Stearns. Some companies that declared bankruptcy were able to restructure rather than be absorbed by different businesses; for instance, the old General Motors revived itself as "the new GM" in 2009.

The collapse of Lehman Brothers resulted in global alarm as stocks around the world plummeted.

sank like a stone. It was a colossal error, and many people said so at the time."

No sooner had Lehman failed than insurance giant AIG began sending out distress signals. The Fed decided it couldn't afford to stand by for this one. Hundreds of firms around the world depended on AIG. The insurer possessed businesses that could be sold for collateral; Lehman had not possessed such collateral. The Fed offered $85 billion. In return, the federal government would take a nearly 80 percent stake in the company. Such a bold move startled many members of Congress. Without any authorization, here was a government agency basically creating money from nothing!

With the stock market still tumbling and everything devaluing, with banks not lending to each other and a run on money markets, the Panic had reached crisis mode. It was time to go to Congress and hope that, even in an election year, they could be convinced to act. It was time to request the authorization of using vast sums of taxpayer money to rescue the banks. It was also time to bring the White House into the game. Before that point, Treasury and the Fed had been keeping the president "informed" but little else. They were running the show. Bernanke and Paulson met with president George Bush on September 18. "When you have the secretary of the Treasury and the chairman of the Fed say, if

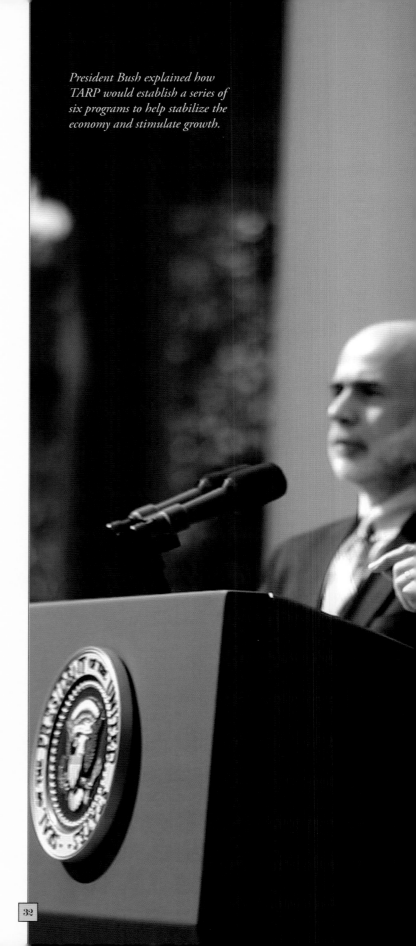

we don't act boldly, we could be in a depression greater than the Great Depression, that's an 'uh-oh' moment," admitted President Bush. The three of them decided they would ask Congress for $500 billion.

The next meeting was on the Hill that night, with Speaker Nancy Pelosi and about a dozen congressional leaders. Bernanke took the lead in explaining the situation. "I kind of scared them," Bernanke later said. "I kind of scared myself." The Troubled Asset Relief Program (TARP) funds ended up being $700 billion, with the first $125 billion going to 9 banks at the end of October.

POINTING OUT

DOWN AROUND THE WORLD

Not only in America did the economic troubles take hold. Greece entered a recession in 2008, and its economy shrank by a quarter. It wasn't until 2014 that Greece came out of the recession. Even then, unemployment was still incredibly high (above 26 percent), and the unrest had spread throughout its political system. Other countries greatly affected by financial weakness included Ukraine, Argentina, Jamaica, Ireland, and Russia. Frustrated citizens gathered in public places to protest against their governments, banking systems, and economic injustices.

CHAPTER FOUR

CRAWLING TOWARD RECOVERY

After the bank bailouts, Wall Street emerged profitable and with larger bank conglomerations than before. Talk about increasing regulations to prevent similar cycles of collapse and bailout from happening in the future resulted in a few new rules, but Wall Street lobbyists kept these at bay. Politicians didn't push for more because "the Street is where the money is."

Throughout the presidential campaign of 2008, candidates had talked about Wall Street versus Main Street. Ordinary citizens who had suffered job and home loss during the recession were not seeing the same types of "bailouts" as the firms on Wall Street. New president Barack Obama signed into law a $787-billion economic stimulus package on February 17, 2009. Composed of tax cuts and spending increases, the plan included funds designated to improve infrastructure, schools, healthcare, and clean energy. It was expected to be doled out over the next 10 years.

A few months into 2009, Bernanke reflected, "The people who were initially saying, 'You should just let these guys fail' have turned their complaint to, 'Well, the government's inconsistent responses have been a

Within a year, the American Recovery and Reinvestment Act of 2009 helped create more than 2 million jobs.

PUTTING AMERICA TO WORK

PROJECT FUNDED BY THE American Recovery and Reinvestment Act

RECOVERY.GOV

FOREST SERVICE US DEPARTMENT OF AGRICULTURE

In December 2015, the Fed raised the federal funds interest rate for the first time since the beginning of the Great Recession.

problem and have prevented recovery.'… My reply to that is twofold. First, we did the best we could with the powers we had. Perfect consistency simply wasn't possible given our limited powers and the differences in the various circumstances. If we had a clear legal framework for resolving big financial institutions other than banks, that would have been a different matter. We didn't have one. Second, the dominant cause of the crisis was not what the Fed did or what other parts of the government did. It was the losses that followed the collapse of the credit boom. When losses pass $1 trillion and continue to rise, one can hardly expect anything other than a worsening situation. It has to be fixed. It will not fix itself."

Although the Great Recession technically ended in June 2009, the unemployment rate continued to rise, peaking at 10 percent in October. Thereafter, it went on the decline. By the end of 2015, it was down to 5 percent—matching the level it had been at the start of the recession in December 2007. Such a slow rebound for both

Demonstrators urged government action as the unemployment rate stayed above 9 percent for more than 2 years.

unemployment and the economy at large spoke to other issues at play. Still, the Fed seemed confident in the U.S. economy's ability to move forward. It announced in December 2015 that it would start raising the federal funds interest rate from zero—a step toward normalcy.

But what is "normal" in the era after the Great Recession? From 2007 to 2010, the national average wage hovered between $40,405 and $41,673; as of 2014, it was $46,481.52, indicating that wage increases are gradually returning. Yet averages often belie the whole story. For lower-income Americans, their household incomes continued to decline after 2009. The richest 1 percent, on the other hand, continued to increase their wealth. As

People who showed up for job fairs were sometimes turned away because so few businesses were hiring.

political economist Robert Reich has observed, "by the end of 2009, most of the rich had bounced back, and the gap between them and everyone else was widening again. One major reason: Most of the assets of rich Americans are held in stocks, **bonds**, and other financial instruments—whose values rose in the wake of the Great Recession as companies cut costs (typically their U.S. payrolls) and expanded their global operations. By contrast,… the major asset of middle-class Americans has been their homes, whose prices took a beating in the downturn and, in most parts of the country, won't return to their 2007 levels for many years."

To offset such losses, Americans might need to get used to a lower standard of living. This is easier said than done; it's harder to give something up than to never have had it in the first place! And middle- and lower-class citizens will likely have to adjust to living at an even more disproportional disadvantage than the very rich. If one of the causes of the Great Recession was excessive spending driven by debt, learning to make do with less seems a practical solution. But what if the broad majority of American workers were able to both spend and save? What if they were given the means to do so by earning (or keeping) more money, thanks to higher wages and lower taxes?

POINTING OUT

NEW RULES FOR FINANCE

On July 21, 2010, President Obama signed the Dodd–Frank Act, the country's biggest financial regulatory overhaul since the Great Depression. Introduced in the House by Massachusetts representative Barney Frank and in the Senate Banking Committee by Christopher Dodd, it was intended to prevent another major crisis—and future bailouts. Among other things, the act brought large nonbank financial organizations under the Fed's oversight. It also attempted to get rid of the too-big-to-fail concept and created the new Consumer Financial Protection Bureau.

In 2011, continued protests against the 2008 bailouts grew into a larger organized movement known as Occupy Wall Street.

I'VE GOT
A 4.0 GPA
$90,000 IN DEBT
& NO JOB.
WHERE IS MY BAIL OUT?

Activists gathered in Germany in June 2015 to implore national leaders to respond to the needs of the world's poor, still in the grip of hardship.

WHO'S RESPONSIBLE?

Many American taxpayers did not take kindly to the Fed's willingness to bail out Wall Street businesses. Using federal money to prop up financial institutions essentially left taxpayers on the hook. And that was an uneasy feeling in such uncertain times. Six months after the Fed took over AIG in September 2008, the public was outraged to learn that the firm was going to award its executives with $165 million worth of bonuses. People wrote threatening letters and traveled by bus to the homes of those executives to let them know how much they disapproved.

The path forward is somewhat unclear. Some of the lessons from the Great Recession may not be fully known until decades down the road. Some are apparent only a few years removed: safeguards for mortgages have been put in place, the Fed's role as "lender of last resort" is still intact, a process for financial firms to be *allowed* to fail is now law, and people realize that national financial problems are really global—often requiring global solutions and support. For the Great Recession ensnared more than just the U.S., and it will take a joint international effort to turn everyone back from the edge of the cliff.

TIMELINE

December 2007	The Great Recession begins. Unemployment is at 5 percent.
January 30, 2008	The Fed lowers the interest rate for the fifth time in four months, bringing it down to 3 percent.
March 16, 2008	JP Morgan announces it will buy out Bear Stearns for $2 per share. Two weeks later, JP Morgan agrees to pay $10 per share.
September 7, 2008	Fannie Mae and Freddie Mac are taken over by the U.S. government.
September 15, 2008	Lehman Brothers files for bankruptcy, the largest case of bankruptcy in U.S. history.
September 16, 2008	To prevent insurance giant AIG from also going under, the Fed bails it out for $85 billion.
October 3, 2008	President George W. Bush signs the Troubled Asset Relief Program (TARP) into law.
October 28, 2008	The first bundle of TARP money ($125 billion) is doled out to 9 banks.
November 23, 2008	Another rescue package is planned, this time to save New York–based bank Citigroup.
December 16, 2008	The Fed lowers the interest rate to zero for the first time in history.
December 19, 2008	Automotive companies General Motors and Chrysler are bailed out with money from TARP.
February 17, 2009	President Barack Obama signs a $787-billion stimulus bill into law.
March 9, 2009	The stock market closes at its lowest point of the recession, at 6,547—54 percent lower than its October 9, 2007, high of 14,164.
June 2009	General Motors files for bankruptcy; later that month, the recession officially ends.

bankruptcy—a situation in which a business (or person) does not have enough money to pay all its debts; when a business files for bankruptcy, it is declared legally unable to pay its debts and is either closed down or reorganized

bonds—documents through which the government or a company promises to pay back money it has borrowed, with interest

commercial—having to do with business; commercial banks take deposits from and make loans to businesses and individuals

credit—money provided by a bank and paid back at a future date

debt ceiling—the maximum amount of money a government may borrow

deflation—a reduction in the general level of prices

derivatives—complex financial contracts

economy—the system through which goods are produced, distributed, and consumed

foreclosure—a legal process in which a bank takes back a home for which the homeowner is unable to make mortgage payments; the bank then tries to sell the home

Great Depression—the decade-long economic downturn that began with the stock market crash of October 29, 1929

inflation—an overall increase in price levels across a wide range of products and services

interest—an amount charged to borrow money; usually the interest charge is a percentage of the amount borrowed

recession—a period during which economic growth slows; recessions are often marked by high unemployment

securities—certificates that show ownership of stocks or bonds

stock—shared ownership in a company by many people who buy shares, or portions, of stock, hoping the company will make a profit and the stock value will increase

Axilrod, Stephen H. *Inside the Fed: Monetary Policy and Its Management, Martin through Greenspan to Bernanke*. Cambridge, Mass.: MIT Press, 2009.

Blinder, Alan S. *After the Music Stopped: The Financial Crisis, the Response, and the Work Ahead*. New York: Penguin, 2013.

Reich, Robert B. *Aftershock: The Next Economy and America's Future*. New York: Knopf, 2010.

Sorkin, Andrew Ross. *Too Big to Fail*. New York: Viking, 2009.

Wessel, David. *In Fed We Trust: Ben Bernanke's War on the Great Panic*. New York: Crown Business, 2009.

Chair the Fed Game
http://sffed-education.org/chairman/
Try your hand at setting the federal funds rate.
Watch how the changes you make affect the economy.

Federal Reserve Bank of Boston: Games and Online Learning
https://www.bostonfed.org/education/online/
Learn more about the economy with games, apps, and quizzes.

Note: Every effort has been made to ensure that the websites listed above are suitable for children, that they have educational value, and that they contain no inappropriate material. However, because of the nature of the Internet, it is impossible to guarantee that these sites will remain active indefinitely or that their contents will not be altered.